AIRBORNE

Poems (1990-1996)

by

Tennessee Reed

Tennessee Reed
January 31, 2004

Raven's Bones Press
Juneau, Alaska

©1996 by Tennessee Reed
All Rights Reserved
First Printing
Printed in the United States of America
ISBN # 0-913666-69
Library of Congress Catalog Card # 96-071120

No part of this book may be reproduced or transmitted
in any form by any means without the written permission
of the publisher

Book edited by Carla Blank
Cover design by Canterbury Press, Berkeley
Cover photo by Susan Lindh
Page composition by Archetype Typography, Berkeley

Raven's Bones Press
320 West Willoughby Ave., Suite 100
Juneau, Alaska 99801

For ordering information contact:
Raven's Bones Press, 872 53rd Street, Oakland, CA 94608

To my grandfather, Bennie Reed, Sr.,

my cousin, Marquel LeNoir,

my dear friend Paul Lofty,

and my cat, Happy,

who have all passed away

while I have been working on this book

Other Books by Tennessee Reed

Circus In The Sky (1988)

Electric Chocolate (1990)

CONTENTS

1990:

My Room Rules	1
The Old Parents Blues	3
Cardiovascular Lesson	5
Human Mine	6

1991:

New Year's Resolution, 1991	7
Sweet Peace for Those in the Middle East	9
Leaving 13 Forever	12
Troubadour Song	14
Summer	16
The Fastest Transportation	17
The House, the Hill, and the Cat	19
Going Back to School Blues	21
Exploring New Worlds	23
Tale of the Tree II	24

1992:

New Year's Resolution, 1992	25
Going Back to Face the Music	27
I Don't Stop When I Play Bebop	30
Eulogy	32

Dear Dad	33
Bad Things, Bad Luck	34
Death Called My Grandfather	35
Beware Do Not Cross the Bear Warning	38
Washington, D.C.	41
I'm Divided	42
If I Could Turn Back Time	43
Hair	45
Check Your Battery	47

1993:

Untitled	49
Naturmuseum, Frankfurt am Main	50
School Spirit	54
Mountain/City	55
Place Names	56
Reverie on Beowulf	58
Today, Sunday	59

1994:

New Year's Resolution, 1994	61
Earth: Third Planet from the Sun	62
Schwarzwald Romantik	64
An Adventure in Romance Form	66
Camp of the Redwoods	71

Queen Bess	72
The Sky's the Limit	75
Untitled	76
Terror Tactics	77

1995:

Pact with the Devil	79
Sorry Sir I Didn't Mean to Shoot You	83

1996:

Study of a Young, Smiling Stewardess	85
Jellies	87
Nihon No Ryori (Japanese Travel)	88
Airborne	91

Ending Poem:

Poems Make Your Life Better	95

About the Author   97

AIRBORNE

MY ROOM RULES

No touching toys or anything else
    without permission.
No bringing food or drinks
    into my room.
Do not use the chalkboard
    unless we are playing school.
Do not write swear words
    on chalkboard.
Do not mess up doll house.
Do not break furniture
    in doll house.
Clean up after yourself
    before you go home.
No going in my desk drawers.
No touching toys on the sixth
    or seventh shelves of white bookshelf
    (because there are precious toys
    from all over the world like Martinique,
        Senegal, Nigeria, Mexico, France,
        Switzerland, Belgium, Germany,
        Italy, Japan, Alaska, New Orleans,
        Peru, Ecuador, Niagara Falls, Canada,
        Russia, China, and Czechoslovakia).

Do not come into my room
without reading this sign
    AND
DO NOT DISTURB
    while
doing homework
writing poems
writing journal
being angry

being sad
playing private things
writing signs
playing with birthday, Chanukah,
Christmas and Halloween presents
me and my friends are playing
    or working
When door is closed
it means DO NOT DISTURB
Do not try to own my room.

Thank you,
Tennessee M.T.T. Reed

P.S.   If you don't read signs
       you mayn't come into my room
       and I mean every word.
       If you read these signs
       you may come into my room.

P.P.S. PLEASE KNOCK

THE OLD PARENTS BLUES

My parents took me to
the movies tonight.
You should have been there.
It was a sight.

It was so funny I cracked up
but then I got the blues.
It was so funny I cracked up
but then I got the blues.

Oh my father forgot
the cinema number.
We had to go back again
and ask the usher.

It was so funny I cracked up
but then I got the blues.
It was so funny I cracked up
but then I got the blues.

When we came home
my mom didn't know
she'd kept her sunglasses on
all through the show.

My mom said, "Did the lights go out?,"
she took off her glasses,
with a hoot and a shout
Dad said, "I wondered what that was all about."

That's why I'm singing this song,
Oh we were cracking up a storm
but then I got the blues

but then I got the blues.

Tell me what's next
as they go into night.
Will they cross the street
with a seeing eye dog
on a red light?

Will they lose the car
forgetting where it's parked?
When they speak, will their words
be off the mark?

but mostly I'm worried,
things going as they can
that maybe
they will forget
who I am.

So that's why I'm singing this song.
Oh we were cracking up a storm
but then I got the blues
but then I got the blues.

CARDIOVASCULAR LESSON

Once I thought
that the heart
was shaped
like the heart
we draw
for Valentines.
And the blood inside
was red
instead
of blue.

Then I asked
if the heart
inside
was like the heart we draw
for Valentines.

And the answer was no,
it looks more like a clenched fist.
But when the blood
inside
hits the oxygen
outside
it turns
from blue
to red.

HUMAN MINE

Some people say
we have earth,
fire, air, and water
in our bodies:
a complete chart of elements.

If an element is one of the parts
that make up a whole
a substance that cannot easily be broken
there is an element of truth to the saying
"Ashes to ashes, dust to dust"
and a reason to discover
the gold and silver
mines that are within.

NEW YEAR'S RESOLUTIONS, 1991

I want to go
to Germany and Czechoslovakia this year
at least those two countries
and all over Central
and Eastern Europe
and go back to Pittsburgh
to swim at the JCC
and to Southern California
and Echo Lake Environmental Camp
(except for the backpacking trip)
again.

I want to get
a whole lot more
jean skirts
and jean jackets
that go with them—
to get a whole bunch of clothes
and let my hair grow.

I want to see
the whole body
put together—
what real people's
arteries and veins look like—
the color
and stuff.

I want to get
my children's book
published.

I would like

to dye my hair black
No,
make that blonde.

I would like to move
to the East Coast
Philadelphia, Pennsylvania
and Cambridge, Massachusetts.

I would like to be
M.C. Hammer,
Winona Ryder,
to join the Ice Capades,
to be on one music video
in a song I like.

SWEET PEACE FOR THOSE IN THE MIDDLE EAST

Peace
for those
in the Middle East

Peace
for those
in the Middle East

My name is
Tiya
and I'd like to say
I like this world
and I know we need to pray
because the world is in a war
in the Middle East
Why can't
George Bush
make up his
mind and give
us some Peace?!

My name is Mani W
and I'd like to say
I like this world
and I know we need to pray
because the world is in a war
in the Middle East
Why can't Saddam Hussein
make up his
mind and give
us some peace?!

Peace
for those

in the Middle
East

I have a color
for this war
and it is red
Red = blood
why can't we
get that in
our heads
That war is
killing innocent
lives with
lots of guns
and lots of knives
we are bombing
Baghdad and Tel Aviv
That isn't right
you see

It's me again
Mani W
you see
That's what's going on
in Baghdad and Tel Aviv
Japan and Germany
are donating planes
everybody is going insane
I think Baker
should have put out a helping hand
when he and Saddam Hussein
met in Geneva, Switzerland

Peace
for those

in the
Middle East

Here's what we have to say
Dear President Bush
I know you're the president and everything
and I'm not trying to be mean or anything
but I think you should get it
through your head
that war is
killing innocent lives
and it won't solve anything
Many people in states, countries and continents
will get killed if
we don't have PEACE!!
If you would look at what's going on
in Baghdad and Riyadh and Tel Aviv
you would see
that I was right
Could you please make peace

Peace
for those
in the
Middle East

Peace
for those
in the
Middle East

Sincerely,

TMT Tia Reed & Mani W
from the Bay Area

LEAVING 13 FOREVER

Leaving 13 forever
going onto 14
in a week and a day
I know what 14 is
in Spanish:
catorce
what's so funny about that?

Now there's 3 days left
and I am getting very happy
to say adios, au revoir, ciao
and good riddance 13
and nervous
because I'm getting older
and older

My first year of teenage life
is over
and 13
is not very nice
for anybody
growing up

I turned 14 today
at 1:26 AM
I woke at 1:35
and stared at the clock thinking
9 minutes ago I left 13

I am so used
to 13
I can't believe
I'm 14

At 3:30 I woke up
and said
this morning takes too long
when is this middle
of the night
going to end
so I can wake up
get dressed
and do
everything
I want to

TROUBADOUR SONG

I've done some travelling
I want to do some more
to go to all the places
I've never been before.
My parents have gone places I never have
that I really wanted to go to so bad.
Like West Germany, Italy, Switzerland, and France,
I don't know if I'll ever have the chance.

I like to go to the East Coast
I've been there eighteen times
or out of the country
I've done that four times
I've been to both the Midwest and Southwest one time,
the Northwest eight times,
and I've been off the Mainland three times.

I have one thing to say
I have been to places different than they.
Like Camp del Vallo in Livermore, California
and Canyon de Chelly in Arizona.

I've been to Maine, Japan, England, Anaheim and Hawaii once
I've been to Illinois, Martinique, Santa Barbara,
Pennsylvania, Washington and Alaska twice.
I've been to New Hampshire and Vermont three times.
I've been to Oregon, Los Angeles and Connecticut four times.
I've been to Massachusetts six or seven times.
I've been to New York fifteen times.

I have been places that my father hasn't been to,
and places that my Mother hasn't been to too.
My father has never been to Maine or Japan,

My mother has never been to Maryland.
But all three of us have been to England.

I have been to the capitol
of every country I've visited:
Tokyo, London, and Fort de France
But I've never been to my own country's capitol
Washington, D.C.
Just been cross the Delaware Bay
in Baltimore, USA.

I've done some travelling
I want to do some more
to go to all the places
I've never been before.
I want to go to Paris, Athens, Rome, and Vienna,
Dublin, Lisbon, Copenhagen, and Geneva,
Berlin, Belgrade, Sofia, Budapest,
Prague, Tirana and Bucharest.

SUMMER

Summer means to me being happy and gay,
where we have no homework and we can play all day.
School is almost out, then we can be in the sun,
go swimming and to camp, and have a lot of fun.
Go traveling to Europe and the East Coast,
and we can have a graduation toast.
So say, "Hear hear!"
and have cheer
because summer is on its way
where we can swim, and have free time all day.

THE FASTEST TRANSPORTATION

I place a map of the world
on the floor
in my living room.
There are arrows on it
and I point out where
I want to
go
on the map.

I shrink to a very small size
and then
slide
on the arrows
until I get to any place
I want to go.

I could do
all the seven continents
in one day
all around the world
to every single country
or
it could take
a long time
like a hundred years.

It's better than taking the plane
and going through all the passports
and international terminals
and landing in rainstorms
and turbulence.

Instead, I slide on an arrow,

like a magic marker carpet
flying faster
than any plane could
take me.

THE HOUSE, THE HILL, AND THE CAT

Square at the bottom,
triangle at the top, the house stands
60 feet high from the ground.
It sits on a slope as the sun goes down,
at 2:59 on a Friday afternoon.
Smoke comes from its chimney.

The hill's great slope
causes the house to look
like it is on a tilt,
but it is not.
The hill is 400 feet high.

The cat, a little Persian calico,
who is two, almost three,
walks in the big backyard,
sniffs the flowers,
and scares the bees.

The house is across the street
from La Loma, the park
with a wooden tower
where at the top you can see the Bay
and a stainless steel automatic bar
that mysteriously slides 10 feet
when someone hangs from its ring.
The cat goes up the house stairs
and peers down at the park.

She sees ghost children
swinging on the swings
and gliding on the automatic bar
and people cheering

at a Little League baseball game.
She meows and shows her fangs
and all the ghosts go away.

That is the story of
the house, the hill,
and the cat.
This is a real house
that I've always wanted
to live in.
And the cat
is my cat.

GOING BACK TO SCHOOL BLUES

Woke up at 4:02
looking at my outfit
that's why I didn't go
back to sleep

Right now I'm trying to eat
can't talk with my mouth full
got to try not to get anything on me
I'm too nervous to eat

First day of high school
hard to think
that I'm
a freshman
2 months of no school
traveling and all that stuff

My stomach hurts
I've stopped eating
I've gotta wash my face
and brush my teeth
that's the last thing I need
toothpaste on my jumper

I'm wearing a white turtleneck
with blue hearts
I'm wearing a blue denim jumper
with black belt
white tights
and some Heather Nakasone originals:
blue tennis shoes with special paint
designs: rollerskates, hearts, cats,
      rainbows, flowers, sunshine,

    peace signs, music notes
    and a cupcake

I have to face all these people
I didn't like last year
saying: "Oh Tennessee you don't match,"
or "Tennessee's back,"
or "Tennessee always smiles and stares like she did last year,"
and try not to cause
a mess
that will get me suspended
which will be kind of difficult
because I said aggressive words
all summer
and I didn't miss anybody
especially when I traveled

8:00 come on
time to depart
8:30 means the end
of my summer vacation
till June 11 of 1992

EXPLORING NEW WORLDS

There are many ways
of exploring new worlds.
When you are exploring new worlds,
you travel to different places and see
new cultures, new cities, new fashions,
that provide new ways of seeing things.

Living is exploring new worlds.
Every time you go through phases of life
baby, child, adolescent, and adult
you are exploring new worlds.
You are learning new ways of life and learning
to survive in the big world
all by yourself.

When you study different things
like animals, music, etc. and so forth
you are exploring new worlds.
Experimenting makes you know
more than you did before.
Which makes you a different person.

When people add new things to the world
the world changes into a new world.

TALE OF THE TREE II

The lights of Heaven shine all over
a palace of the eldest crane
and all over the welcoming
sky. 7 cranes fly through daylight
and evening, past the sun and moon to
visit the eldest crane. They fly up
and up past the golden cat, the
basket of fruit, the Cheshire cat,
still mischievous, past the acorn and the birds.
They enter the palace of the
eldest crane made by good luck charms
and hearts in a pattern. They give the
eldest crane the 7 good luck wishes:

    Bird 1:   I wish you love
    Bird 2:   I wish you the golden light
    Bird 3:   I wish you no fear
    Bird 4:   I wish you the wings of power
    Bird 5:   I wish you the night
    Bird 6:   I wish you to fly anywhere you like
    Bird 7:   I wish you the 7 good charms

God bless you cranes, birds, God bless you
Cheshire cat, sun, moon, God bless you
basket of fruit and acorn and golden
cat.

Merry Christmas to you all and Happy New
Year!

NEW YEAR'S RESOLUTION, 1992

I know some things I'm gonna do
in 1992:
1. perform my poems at the Bay Area Dance Series
2. go to Germany
3. go camping this summer
4. finish the 9th grade at New Age Academy
5. start 10th grade at Arrowsmith

Here's some things I want to do
in 1992:
1. go to France and Italy during my stay in Germany
2. go to Washington D.C. and New York again
3. go to Dance Camp
4. help save the world
5. have a good year at Arrowsmith
6. change my attitudes toward people my own age
7. write songs and make an album
8. grow my hair out and I don't want
    to dye it black or blond
9. go to Alaska, but this time the Mainland
    and go to Denali and Kautmai National Parks
    and Preserves
10. go to Yellowstone and Yosemite National Parks
    because I haven't been to any national parks
    in California and I haven't been to the Rockies
    or Idaho, Wyoming, and Montana
11. go to Rhode Island, because that's the only state
    in New England that I haven't been to yet
12. be a globe traveler—travel everywhere
13. I want to buy a white outfit so that I can paint on it
    with my new fabric paints

I know I won't get to do most of these things:
      (9)   I probably won't go to Alaska's mainland
      (10) I probably won't go to Yellowstone or Yosemite
      (11) I probably won't go to Rhode Island
      (13) but I will be able to buy a new white outfit

I don't know about (6): changing my attitude
but I'll try by being an individual
and not caring what other people think
about me
and I'm going to pick up all the litter
I find on the ground
and not use anything toxic
to be a part of (4): saving the world

and I'll be fifteen
when I'm doing
all this

GOING BACK TO FACE THE MUSIC

Going back to face the music
yeah

you know what I'll do
if

he says
I act
like a little
kid
all the time
so he can
not even talk

that's a good one
that he can fix
cause he fixes everything

or if
he makes fun
of the way I dance
he'd better think again

he won't get along
in the art world
I'm very sorry to say
if he thinks
there's only one way of doing things
nobody's going to accept him
and he'd better not say
that I didn't warn him
and if he doesn't
get accepted

I'll be up there
rolling on the floor
and saying
that's his little red wagon
cause he ain't gonna
get along in the world
and I'll go on
my merry way

and you know what
I'll do
if
he sexually harasses me?
I'll tell him
he's just telling me
his experience

and her
telling me
I smile too much
and my friends
laughing
at me

just because
they want
to be a part
of the crowd
and they don't know
who they are
and I know
who I am

well I'll tell you something
they ain't my friends
no more

excuse me for xxxxzz!!
they'll go
Uh Ah Uh Ah
I don't think so
I'm not messing
with her today

they better know
who they are

anyway
it's history. . . .
I'm back in the saddle again

I DON'T STOP WHEN I PLAY BEBOP

I play bebop
music by Thelonious Monk
and Miles Davis mostly

"Misterioso"
"Straight, No Chaser,"
"Nutty"
"Just A Gigolo,"
"Let's Cool One,"
"Blues Five Spot,"
and "Four"

It feels weird
I don't know
it just does
seem weird

I don't even
know
if I like playing bebop

But
I learned it
and
like listening
to it
and like
playing it
fast
along with Miles
and Monk
just for the fun
of it

Bebop is a word
Louis Armstrong made up
to put down stuff
younger people
just made up

So I know I'm not
the only one
who gets put down
about new stuff
but I can't stop
trying
new stuff
or bebop a
rebop
bam boom

EULOGY

February 14, 1992

Dear Paul,

The new finish you put on the dining room table still looks good.
We had to give up on the chairs. The mending didn't hold.
But I'm taking care of my Sombrero that you gave me.
I only wear it when I play around.
Do you remember Happy, our cat?
You two got along well. You put her on the special "Paul Lofty" diet.
She is much fatter now.

I hope you are over your cancer and diabetes.
Are you in heaven starting a new Good Life?
Are you having any upcoming concerts at Heaven's Grand Hall?
Will you please sponsor us for complimentary tickets?
We'll be listening. We wouldn't miss it for the world.

Goodbye from,
    Tennessee
    Carla
    Ishmael

P.S. I wrote this poem myself (Tennessee)

DEAR DAD

On the occasion of your fifty-fourth birthday
I want to say
Good Luck
because you're getting up there
and
you're still going on strong
and
you're still traveling around the world
with poetry

And I want to ask
if you're going to write
a poem for fifty-four
like you did for thirty-five
because
I want to know
if you're looking forward
to it
or not

and I want to wish you
a Happy Birthday
and a happy life
all year
and may you
still go on
with your teaching
and poetry

And don't forget
my birthday
is six days
later

BAD THINGS, BAD LUCK

Why me?
Why at this
particular
time?

I think I have 7 years of bad
luck after breaking
two juice
squeeze bottles.

I got a head
cold.
What will
happen next?

Hmmmm.
I have
two sore
muscles.
I banged my
knee.

I could
worry
myself
to death.

DEATH CALLED MY GRANDFATHER

In 1988
when my parents went to Europe
I visited my grandparents in Buffalo.
My cousin, little Vincent,
was two years old.
Little Vincent is something else.
You can't tell he has heart trouble.
He started hitting on me
and then my Grandfather said,
"Keep it up and I'll whip you."
(That was a threat, not a promise.)

Little Vincent started
hitting on him
and then my Grandfather went
looking for a belt
and he said
he couldn't find it.

I was upstairs in my room
and it was so hot
that I couldn't go to sleep
and I was reading "Superfudge,"
the part where Peter's brother, Fudge, was missing
and Fudge's bird, who was named Uncle Feather,
said "Bonjour, stupid,"
and Peter said, "Oh, shut up."
Uncle Feather said, "Shut up yourself, yourself, yourself,"
and I ran down the stairs, cracking up.

I was hyper, I don't know why.
I think it must be the Buffalo weather,
and I read Grandpa the story

and after that
Grandpa always answered the phone
when I would say "Hello,"
with "Shut up yourself, yourself, yourself,"
and we'd giggle together.

Death called my grandfather
cause he had cancer
in his lungs
and his stomach.
(This was real, not fake.)

When I saw him next,
he was in a coffin
with a new suit on
and his face made up.
I remember that.

I remember
when we got there,
the night before the funeral,
I was tired from traveling
but I couldn't sleep
because I was nervous
and I was in a strange place
and it was totally black
so I couldn't see
anything.

I remember the minister
preaching about the Lord.
He said, "Death is not a stop.
It's a yield sign."

And getting my suede shoes

messed up
in the yucky mud
of the graveyard.

And everybody standing
under umbrellas
on a cold wintry day
listening to what
the preacher was saying:
"Ashes to ashes
dust to dust."

The last thing I remember
of my grandfather
is standing by his coffin
and walking back
to the black limousine
to ride back to the church
with my 5 cousins,
his grandchildren.

BEWARE DO NOT CROSS THE BEAR WARNING

If you camp in any national park
on the west side
of the North American continent
beware,
especially during drought
season, of grizzly bears.

They usually stay
in the National Parks
of Wyoming, Washington, Montana,
Alaska and Idaho.

If you come into
their territory
they will attack
because you
are in
their space.

Grizzly bears get really hungry
and they can forage
into your food
especially at night
time when you are sleeping.

Their claws are two inches
long
for digging up
ground squirrels,
their favorite
meal.

They have flat teeth

for eating plants
and they have really sharp
canine fangs
sharper than human's
for cutting up
raw meat
and humans
are raw meat.
They often come with their cub
because, think about it,
their cub needs to eat too.

They are called omnivores
because they eat both
plants and meat.

If you see one
don't panic.
Shout
or throw rocks
at the bear,
and it will go away.

If you shoot them
and they get wounded,
they attack
and pounce on you
and you
are one
dead
sucker.

Like that camper
in 1971
who got killed

by a mother
grizzly in Yellowstone
National Park. The first
time in thirty years.

Or some guy
who got inside
the grizzly's territory
in Alaska,
summer of '91
and the grizzly ate
his ear off.

Also in Alaska,
that same summer
a grizzly was charging
a guy
and the guy got on the ground
and the grizzly ran
right over him.

Just goes to show
you never know
what a grizzly
will do:
charge
or run
away.

WASHINGTON, D.C.

Home of the nation's
business. Home of laws
and the Congress. Home
of the New World Order.
Home of the great airports
Dulles Int'l and Washington
National. Founded by George
Washington and the permission
of Maryland to take its land.
Home of the Kitty Hawk the
Wright Brothers flew located
at the National Air and Space
Museum. Washington. District of
Columbia.

You can get Pecan Pie at the
Holiday Inn. You can sit in a
taxi with a t.v. in the front
going to the airport. You can
get Merry-Go-Round rides at
the park across the street from
the Smithsonian Gift Shop.
You can fly in and out of the
airports every hour. Washington.
District of Columbia.
You can buy a Congressman's votes.

I'M DIVIDED

Like East
and West Berlin
before unification
a wall separates
my body from
my mind
and I don't
want to chip
away at the wall

I try to convince
myself
that I'm not
at war with
myself
(but there I go
again, bumping myself
off
even now)

IF I COULD TURN BACK TIME

If I could turn back time
I wouldn't have ear infections and my ears would be
pierced for a long time

If I could turn back time
I would have long hair all my life

If I could turn back time
I would go to Europe with my parents on every trip

If I could turn back time I wouldn't have
measles, lice, or the stomach flu

If I could turn back time
there wouldn't be a hole
bigger than Europe in the ozone layer by Antarctica

If I could turn back time
I would ban people cutting down forests

If I could turn back time
people would be kind and not kill animals
to wear their skins

If I could turn back time
there would be world peace

If I could turn back time
there wouldn't be global warming

If I could turn back time
all the extinct animals like
the saber-tooth tiger, the mammoth, dodo bird,

Tasmanian wolf, mountain gorilla,
and the quagge
would be
alive again

If
I could
turn
back

HAIR

It's an important issue
as you can see
I have a thing about it
it's part of my image
I used to have really short hair
when I lived up in Seattle
which I hated
because you can't do
hairstyles
with it
now I'm going to cut
the back
when the front gets
to my shoulders
which seems like it's going
to take forever
I'll probably be in college by then
except it probably won't
because my hair grows
really fast
now I wear hair scrunchies
to match my outfit
and keep my hair
out of my face
my plan is
to grow my hair
to my waist
and braid it
and put it in a bun
and a pony tail
and stuff like that
to look like a 1950's moderne dancer
and my plan it to never

wear it down
because my hair poufs out
really ugly looking
like electricity shocked my hair into standing up on end
like the Bride of Frankenstein's
or cut it short
again

CHECK YOUR BATTERY

I don't want to think today
my skull is so hollow
it makes a funny sound
when I bang on the top
until after a while
it starts hurting.

I must look like a fool
the way I'm clunking on my head
with my mouth
making fish lips
to change the sound.

I can do Beethoven's Fifth
dot dot dot doooot
and Clemente's scales
move my brain in eighth note time.

I'm just wondering
what does it mean
if it makes those sounds?

That there is nothing
in my head?
Or is my brain so much smaller
than my skull
that it slipped
into the back
of my neck?

That would be good
because the brain would be protected
in case

a coconut fell on top
of my head since
the longer the fall
the bigger the dent.

Check your battery
See if you need
some internal surgery
on your head
giving a new charge
to turn on your light bulb.

Like a black hole in outer space
I suck in mischief

until there is no room
to store it
anymore

NATURMUSEUM, FRANKFURT AM MAIN

I saw a class earlier
I bumped into them
in the room with the dinosaurs
and they all stared at my black
denim jumper like it was exciting.

The teacher said something to me
I don't know what it was
but I think she told me off
because she sounded hyped up,
serious and mad.
I was just sitting there
minding my business
on the bench with my Mom
talking about some dinosaur, Rexy,
Tyrannosaurus Rex.

I saw them again, sitting on the floor.
The teacher was sitting with her hands on her knees,
her head bobbing
duf duf duf duf duf duf duf duf
to each kid.
Her earrings jiggled every move she made.
She was talking in German.
I don't know German,
but that's what it sounded like.

A boy was sitting cross legged
on the floor
probably grinning at her,
I didn't see his face though,
but the teacher had this serious look
on her face.

I wonder why?

The boy had brown eyes and brown hair.
The teacher had blonde hair and blue eyes.
I really examined them.
The teacher was wearing
this blouse that was tied at her midriff
and tight jeans.
You'd have to walk like a robot they were so tight.
I'd never seen a teacher in jeans so tight before.
That was new. And she had sandals on.
The boy was wearing a white collar shirt and blue shorts
white socks and sneakers
cause it was hot.
One of the girls had pink on, a skirt and a shirt with sandals
with blonde hair and blue eyes also.
She wore her hair in a ponytail and a pink hair tie
and she looked at me with wide eyes.

And then we left the room, looking for something to eat
but it was too hot to eat pizza
which was all I liked
of what they served at the museum
so we decided to leave
and there was the boy
again
with a goofy grin on his face
like Mickey Mouse
his eyes were wide and
his teeth were showing.

That picture keeps coming
to my mind
and I wonder
why I am so interested

in that boy
who looked so excited
in a calm sort of way
coming out of the museum
probably thinking about
what he saw
a dead animal
who would be excited
about a dead animal?

And I ask
where the boy is now
sleeping or something
and does the teacher snore
with a German accent?

The same event: my dream version

On May 25th of 1992
I was in Germany in
this city called Frankfurt am Main.
I was visiting the Naturmuseum Senckenberg on Senckenberganlage.
It was the day I went to Berlin.
I was in the room with the dinosaurs.
There was a boy and girl who were
staring at my Guess "Made in USA" jumper
I got at Hilltop Mall in Richmond, California.
I did an eye performance for them:
I rolled my eyes to the ceiling
I crossed them and rolled them
from side to side.
The teacher and the other kids stared.
I said, "See ya, wouldn't wanna be ya."
Then I left the room.

I saw them again, sitting on the floor
praying that they didn't see me
because I made a fool of myself.
The boy was going outside, smiling maybe
he was excited about what he saw, maybe not.
Anyway he glanced at me.
I said "Guten Tag."
He looked away.
I said "Anyway."
He looked at me.
I said "I said 'anyway.'
Do you have a problem with that?"
He looked at me still.
I said "Auf wedersehn"
and left.

SCHOOL SPIRIT

Blue whales have hearts
the size of a car
and eyes the size of a basketball
at 100 feet in length
and 150 tons
unchallenged
they could toss a football
from their tails to their heads
and score a goal
for their school

MOUNTAIN

I see the trees
I hear the crickets
I smell the flowers
I touch the leaves

CITY

I see the people
I hear the traffic
I smell the bad air
I touch the cement

PLACE NAMES

Place names call
up memories of places
I've been to

and collected
on my clothes like:
    Amsterdam Holland
        with the two lions
        and crown of their crest
    New York Memories: Central Park,
        Statue of Liberty, Fifth Avenue,
        Soho, and the Chrysler Building

or been gifted:
    "I left my heart in Cleveland"
    "Citta Del Mia Corre, Lugano"
    "No Brand Art" from Detroit, the Motor City

or places
that everybody else has
the name of like "Universite Paris Sorbonne"

or even labels that say "Made in USA," and

I have my pink Euro joy warm-up suit
    made in Milano
black sheer stockings
    made in Granada, Mississippi
abalone shell earrings
    made in India
black sandals
    made in Tunisia
ankle socks with heart designs

    made in Germany
blue jean shorts with embroidered pockets
    made in Sri Lanka
hot pink and turquoise jacket
    made in Indonesia
white lace and gems T-shirt
    made in China
wild painted leggings
    made in England
slippers and pajamas
    made in the Philippines
black boots
    made in Brazil
hair elastics and roller skates
    made in Taiwan
black blouse with white polka dots
    made in Korea
red turtleneck
    from Hong Kong

just getting dressed in the morning
makes me feel
like I'm a world traveler

REVERIE ON BEOWULF

From the beginning of Europe
came a really dark feeling
telling of feudal knights
and foolhardy monsters
locked in rousting feats
to the death

We call their names:
Beowulf, heroic thane from Sweden
Hrothgar, old king of Denmark
Hygelac, uncle to Beowulf and king of Geats
Wiglaf, Beowulf's bravest thane
Unferth, who gave his hrunting to Beowulf
Queen Wealtheow, beloved wife of Hrothgar
Ugly Grendel, cursed heathen cannibal
Grendel's Mother, monster of a woman
and the unnamed dragon, a fire breathing beast

Three marauding malevolent monsters
slain by the hero
to bring accord
to the avenged
land of Denmark
so that veiled Europe
and monotheism's rise
could be celebrated on the pyre
of loneliness and depression

TODAY, SUNDAY

Today, Sunday
the twenty-seventh of December,
was supposed to
be Marquel's birthday.

The weather fit the day:
gray, gloomy, cold;
Marquel was supposed to
be nineteen.

She died November 6, 1992
in a car accident.
This was in Hampton, Virginia
where she was a freshman
pre-Med student in college.

There were 4 passengers in the car
when the driver fell asleep
and the car crashed into a tree.
The other 4 lived,
but Marquel died.

We can't say whose fault it was,
but the driver must feel
really scared and guilty.

I remember the day of the funeral.
We went into the Oakland hills,
trying to find the Church.
Instead, we found burnt down houses.

When we found Lake Temescal,
we knew we were going the right way.

The Church was so crowded
we had to stand up for a long time.

When her best friend spoke about her
and began to cry,
I started to cry.

We got lost
two more times that day.
We went straight
from school to her house,
going down Thornhill
trying to find Mountain Boulevard
and going up and down and up Snake Road
onto Manzanita Drive.

We watched *Cinderella*
with two kids,
Marquel's cousins,
named Brianna and Jordan.
I talked to them
and ate dinner.
Then we drove back home.

Now when I work
at my Uncle's doctor office,
she won't be there
typing on the computer
and talking on the phone.
It will be so weird.

NEW YEAR'S RESOLUTION, 1994

to grow my bangs out
to clear the acne on my forehead
to wear pants and shorts to school always
to go to Europe and Asilomar
to travel on a lot of airplanes
to get more Guess? clothes
to see more movies
to get more hair stuff and earrings
to take Driver's Ed during the summer
to let my hair get half way down my back
    without cutting the split ends off
to relax my hair every six to nine months
    instead of every three months
to do well on my tests and finals
to try to talk back to kids who are rude to me
to see my friends outside of school
    and call them more often
to keep myself in great health
to stop complaining and worrying so much
to act more 17.

January 9, 1994
my first poem of 1994, everybody

EARTH: THIRD PLANET FROM THE SUN

I heard that countries
on the Equator
have vivid sunsets

I saw Greenland's sunrise
going from JFK
to Amsterdam

The sky was green
a vivid green
I can't name the shade of it

I feel part of the solar system
flying in the sky
unlike when I'm on the ground
because I am off
the ball

Noah's dad told me
that the earth expands
in the middle

Going over Greenland
to get to Europe
is faster than going across the Atlantic

When you're on Earth
you are tilting sideways
along with the buildings, streets, and forest

When you loop
on an airplane and land
you land vertical

instead of horizontal

Well it depends
actually
on which direction
you are coming from

SCHWARZWALD ROMANTIK

>upon reading Marvell's *Garden*

Black Forest,
a romantic forest
situated in the Alps
of Germany

Black Forest,
a breath taking
enchantment,
the most lovely
forest on the planet

the asparagus
fresh from the
ground with cream
or cheese

tree covered mountains
hiding houses and restaurants,
hang gliders,
tourists,
and residents
above one of
Germany's
picture postcard perfect towns,
Frieburg

Schwarzwald Romantik,
I love you, if I could
only go back again
eat your asparagus,
breathe your air

Schwarzwald Romantic
thank you from
the bottom of
my heart

AN ADVENTURE IN ROMANCE FORM

*This story takes place
in the Museum of Natural History—*
a place for contemplating the story of nature
which is another way to say
it is the story of learning
from innocent forces in the universe—
that's why it's called by its name.

My quest: to find out if I could survive in nature
by seeing how animals lived in the past:
because we all have to
survive
to tell our story.

One day after the museum had closed,
and no one was there to stop me,
I touched a black marble stone
set in the floor.
On my touch, the glass dissolved
on a nearby diorama,
the one that holds the mountain lions.

This is an animal of many names: American lion, cougar,
deer tiger, Mexican lion,
painter (a corruption of panther),
panther, mountain lion, catamount. (*Felis Concolor*)
The Incas of Quechuan named it Puma.
You know that an animal must be powerful
if it has earned so many names.

Puma was not found in the Old World.
Puma is a New World animal
the biggest cat in the Americas,

except for the jaguar,
a god of the Mayans,
a cat who comes out
of the era of the fourth sun,
the era before ours.

Puma once prowled North and South America,
as far north and east as Maine,
from British Columbia to Patagonia,
living in cold high mountains, and hot deserts and jungles.

Pumas like to sharpen their claws on trees.
While traveling their territory,
hunters can tell
which way they go
by reading paw marks
facing the opposite direction
of the way the cats travel.

Pumas are good stalkers of wild game like
rabbit squirrel, wapiti and deer
and domestic animals like sheep and cattle
which caused the pioneers to call them
a threat.

Puma may be the only large cat
that rarely kills men
and still survives.

The Natural History pumas live forever
by Shiva's temple,
a flat-topped butte
dotted by Mountain Mahogany,
Sea of Cactus and Cliff Rose
on the North Rim of the Grand Canyon

looking South
from Point Sublime.

On ears-up alert,
the male sits on his haunches
looking across the tableland;
the female rests on her side,
with back to the canyon divide,
and head cocked.

I had been taught the do's and don'ts
for human behavior in cougar country:
    do not approach cougars
        they avoid confrontation
    do not run
        cougars instinctively chase anything that runs
    do not move in ways that can appear animal-like:
        cougars think
        anyone crouching or bending
        may be a meal
    Instead, convince them that you are not prey
        by trying to make yourself appear larger
        by making eye contact,
        throwing stones,
        or anything else you can reach
        without crouching or turning your back
    If attacked, remain standing, face the animal
        and fight back with any means you have,
        including your fists

So from all these warnings
I knew to approach the cats
by walking slow and tall,
talking my intent,
my idea to jump off

the edge of the divide
and run around the canyon floor
letting them hear
I wanted to know
what was on
the bottom.

They watched me
as I crashed into a wall
of painted illusion
on a level plane.

Here I sat face to face
with a man-made universe
of stuffed hides
no organs
no depth
and silence.

I sat there stunned
until I felt the big cat
lick my cheek
and nudge me to the canyon's ledge
where I looked down to see
the canyon floor
rocky edged
and the great red
Colorado River.

I bent my knees, with feet together
lifted my arms above my head
and dove into the river.
I landed safely
unlike the Indian
whose story I heard:

he fell
"like scrambled eggs"
to feed the rocks.

I felt sure
that I wasn't going to be like him
because of my guardian lions' protection
and the invincible cat power
they passed to me
for my swim in the waters
of the river.

I didn't know
it was going to be a strong current
a rushing river that once cut these gorges
through the oldest known rocks
of the earth's crust
through the sedimentary rocks
that form the high walls of the Grand Canyon.

Its rapids still held their rip-roaring speed
that spun me like a top
and tossed me away
back into the Museum of Natural History
back to civilization.

But first,
I passed through the case,
the diorama of the mountain lions,
who licked me clean
to prepare me to go on
into the full light
of understanding nature's power
to give and take life.

CAMP OF THE REDWOODS

Gentle Santa Cruz mountains of the Coastal Range
ancient redwoods grown in fairy rings
smells of pine needles
tall grasses and dazzling blue skies

Camp of the Redwoods
where I did go
to Dance
Camp in August

We'd dance around
the fairy rings
in the meadow
at the rifle range
and inside the summer lodge

Chant "I Walk in Beauty"
listen to flute music
eat in the wood beamed dining hall
and walk in the night time forest

Create water ballets in the
YMCA swimming pool
share space with the
Asthma and Lung Cancer kids' camp
gather leaves in the meadow to make a piece
and sing rounds as we danced trios

Camp of the Redwoods
my favorite camp site

QUEEN BESS

> "I refuse to take no for an answer."
> —*Bessie Coleman*

I had a dream
that I went to Paris in 1921
to see Bessie Coleman
speak about earning her license
at the Federation Aeronatique
Internationale and she took me for a ride
flying in a W. W. I surplus aircraft

I was a woman
about in my 30's
and I was proud
that Bessie was the first
African American
man or woman pilot
to earn a license

This took place in
Paris when Bessie was
in her thirties because
schools in the U.S.
would not let her
earn a license

It was amazing
that a manicurist
born and raised in Texas
who studied French in Chicago
had followed her dream
to become an aviator

I could see her:
she had her goggles
on her head
she had a French cut
sports coat
leggings and black
long lace boots
she had a concentrated
look on her face
like the photo
that appeared on her license

She had to come to me
in my dreams
because the white
media wrote her out of history

Amelia Earhart called herself
"a sack of potatoes"
behind the wheel
because she never
flew the plane for real
yet she was considered
a great heroine
who I heard about in school for years
there was even a picture of
Amelia Earhart in the
principal's office
at a school I attended
because she was white

Bessie was black

But if I had known
about Bessie earlier

I would have
had another influence
to make sure that by my 30's
I'd "amount to something"
to fly in my dreams

THE SKY'S THE LIMIT

I don't know where
we were going
but my Mom pointed out
there was a shadow
of our plane
on a cloud

So I started looking out
of the window
I think the plane
was either a DC-10
or a 747

There was patchy cloudiness
outside but otherwise mostly
sunny
you could see little bits
and pieces of land

I couldn't see the shadow
but I noticed a rainbow
it formed a big arc
that reached out from under the clouds
looped up over the plane
and then disappeared under the clouds again

The plane flew through the rainbow
on its way to our destination

I know the flow of the blood
I know what the love dove is
How it goes
Up to seven quarts
From the vena cava
To the heart
Heart smart,
Get it!

TERROR TACTICS

What a shame!
Tennessee born Ku Klux Klan's grandchildren
went to the house next door
and set a burning cross in Fremont
thinking that it was a black person's family
when it was a white person's family.

5 feet of fire on a green lawn
brought an ancient practice from the Scottish highlands
carried to America by Thomas Dixon,
author of *The Clansmen,*
the romantic novel D.W. Griffin used to make
Birth of a Nation.

The early Klan, inspired by
the Knights of the Round Table
dressed in long hooded robes
(usually white or black
but sometimes red, yellow, or brown)
which covered all of them
except for their eyes.
They even dressed their horses
in robes.

The Klan in the 1860's
burned 13 to 14 foot wood crosses
and if they had no lumber to burn
they put coffins in front of people's houses
or tied people up with cords and drowned them
or hung them from a tree.

Dead bodies
floating down the blood red river

or sprouting as strange nocturnal fruit:
a message to run people out of the county.

Why did they come
across the Southeastern United States
up North to Nebraska and Idaho,
and West to California
to settle in the 1994 computer swollen valley suburb
of Fremont?

Ku Klux means "band" or "circle" in Greek
and a Klan is a family tree.
This family travels in groups of 50 to 75 people,
their protection against an enemy of one.
How would you like to be the one?

PACT WITH THE DEVIL

I walked through the woods
leaving my life in the town behind
I was afraid of the dark
and the tight space
afraid of the unknown

I walked with my friends
we were all African American
runaway slaves
women who wanted to be free
of Baltimore's grasp
so we followed the call of our husbands
who had taken the journey
to Canada
before us

Everywhere was woods then
there was no escape from the trees
we had to pass
through the woods
called the Devil's woods
as we headed North through Buffalo
to Canada

We believed in the Devil
a white slavemaster who lived in the trees
with big eyes and a laughing red face

We knew
the Devil followed us
through his woods
because he lighted our way with his gleaming red eyes
and cleared a trail with his arrow-shaped tail

The woods were endless
so we needed rest
and a way
to stay inside
because the cold had come
and we could travel
no further

We all agreed
with the Devil
to give up our souls
for a cabin of wooden logs
something that was part
of the Devil
for something that was part
of us

So we rested in the cabin
and warmed our forgotten souls
until a while later
when a fierce white man
on a wild white horse appeared
at our door

He dragged us to where the Devil
was standing like an ancient oak tree
waiting for us

He said we'd taken something
that was part of him—
that was his own wood—
and now he wanted it back
to feel complete

But we weren't ready to give the wood back

because it was still winter
time and the cold
kept us
wanting to be
inside

He pointed to thundery clouds
at flashes of lightning
and the crack of thunder

The lightning flashed faces
of our husbands
their faces and beards
extending out as the North Wind
calling to us
this would be our fate, too

We ran back
into the log house
which disintegrated
turning us invisible
the moment we reentered
the Devil's space

We all whirled up to the clouds
joining the North Wind
traveling Northwest
strangely, still
following the route
we had set to Canada

Our bodies flew up in the sky
but our souls remained on the ground
rooted forever
in the Devil's woods

This story took place in Baltimore
during the 1860s
I can tell this tale
because I was once
one of these women
heading toward Buffalo
to escape through
Niagara Falls
to Canada

SORRY SIR I DIDN'T MEAN TO SHOOT YOU

If I were drafted to fight a war
I might shoot my friend instead of the enemy
I might get my leg amputated
and live my life in a wheelchair
or have to walk around
with a big fat hole
in my face
where my nose
used to be
and everyone would stare at me,
like huh?

My daughter could get a hare lip
because I breathed in too much
radiation
or leukemia
from the Agent Orange
I sprayed on trees.

I might leave behind
land mines
or shrapnel bombs
that five years later
fly into bodies
for the rest of their lives.

I could be guilty
of killing an innocent
child's mother
as they went
on their way
to the grocery store,
or accidentally

a bomb could fall
out of my plane
onto farmer's cattle.

And I could get Post Traumatic Stress
Syndrome
that drives me crazy
with memories
of all the vertebrae, blood and guts
spread all over the ground
of what someone once called
their home.

STUDY OF A YOUNG, SMILING STEWARDESS

In an American Airlines ad
that appears on CNN
A young stewardess
walks down the gateway.
With a curious frown,
she's looking at airplanes
parked at the gates.
She is like the woman
in *Portrait of Victorine Meurent*
by the painter Edouard Manet.

The plane takes off.
It's a DC-10.

Segue to inside the cabin.
A little girl kneels in her mom's lap,
held close and tight
as she looks over the back of a seat.
The mother and daughter are right out of
Madonna of the Chair by Raphael.
Her mother is pointing at something
as they sit and talk
by the window.

The young stewardess appears again
smiling at all the passengers
like the woman in Pontormo's
Portrait of a Young Woman.

Segue to outside, in a heavenly blue sky.
The American Airlines plane is flying,
like the angel in *A Maiden's Dream,*
by Lorenzo Lotto.

Segue again to the plane's interior.
A man and a woman
holding hands
like *The Arnolfini Marriage* by Jan Van Eyck.
The stewardess is smiling at them
like the woman in *The Magdelen* by
Bernadino Luini.

The screen turns black.
Ad copy rolls in white
as a piano continues to play
the advertising jingle.

I wish I'd meet this stewardess
with her inviting smile
who fooled me into thinking
I would find her in real life.

I found her in a movie,
called *Baby's Day Out*.
She played a mother
looking for her baby
who had memorized the images
in a book
and traveled
all over town
looking for the images
just like I traveled
over four centuries
to find images
in the world's museums
that matched
that perfect world.

JELLIES

I'm still buying jellies
eight festive, bright pairs:
magenta fisherman's style by Grendha
gold Greek sandal style jellies
by Fashion Steps from Marshall's
clear with a plastic buckle
by Jellisy Footwear from Payless Shoe Source
and clear clunky heels by
Guess Footwear from Macy's
slip-on fisherman sandals
by Glacier Bay from Clothestime
and clear basketweave t-strap sandals
with a purple tint
by Yasmine from Yasmine
and gold sparkly platforms by Jellybeans from Shoe Pavilion.

In Japan, I checked from Fukuoka to Otaru
and resisted all
the choices in plastics—
even the ones decorated with daisies that kept catching my eye—
because they didn't fit
or were cheaper at home.

I'm at my all time high
even though I have this many pairs
when I go into stores I head straight
for the jellies department.

NIHON NO RYORI
(JAPANESE TRAVEL)

You can't always take the airline
you want to take like American or TWA
sometimes you have to take whatever's cheaper
like United or Northwest

You can't always
sit by the window
on the airplane
sometimes you have to sit
by the aisle or
in the middle

You can't always get
American food
like hamburgers, pizza
eggs, and ham
sometimes you can
only eat Japanese food like
sushi, teriyaki, sunomono, and chawanmushi

You can't stay in one place
all of the time
sometimes you have to Shinkansen to or from
a new city daily
like Osaka or Tokyo

You can't always find clunky heeled loafer
Japanese school girl shoes
in your size in Kobe or Kyoto
sometimes you have to go to Nagoya
to find them

You can't always rely on following the schedule
like when I was told
we would go exploring in the morning
or eat at a certain restaurant
sometimes you have to accept
last minute change
like when our guide decided to choose
a restaurant where we sat on tatami mats
instead of a Chinese restaurant
where we could sit on chairs, like at home

You can't get a hotel room
with a big space like the Rihga Royal in Hiroshima
you sometimes have to stay in a tiny
hole-in-the-wall
like the Personal Hotel
in Fukuoka, where the price is good

You won't find the U.S.
everywhere
but you will find courteous people everywhere
safe streets and subways at night
full of people having fun
the walking signal on traffic lights
     playing "Coming Through the Rye"
and 1001 golden visions at Sanjusangendo
moats surrounding the walls of Nijo Castle
red, yellow, or white triangles
     on selected windows
      of high rise glass skyscrapers
the mixture of gray rock, raked granite
     and luscious green gardens
     at the Silver Pavilion
the stork, with his beak striped in pastels
     like a Richard Diebenkorn painting

as he stares from a rock at the Miyajima Aquarium
and a herd of deer following you, asking to be fed
on the beach at the Itsukushima Shrine

AIRBORNE

I like to fly better than taking
cars, boats, trains, and buses
because flying is safer, faster, and
more fun

767s, DC-10s, L1011s . . .
anything but commuter planes
American, Delta, TWA . . .
anything but being cramped and uncomfortable

When I fly it's usually
over the
continental United States
but I've also flown to
Alaska, Hawaii, the Caribbean,
Europe, and Japan

I love to get the window seat
and see the clouds, the sun,
and sometimes rainbows too,
but most of all I like to see
that land is a live
topography map
I don't like to sit
by the aisle or
in the middle

I prefer flying at night
and also at sunrise and sunset
because I feel more part of the solar system
even though I'm still in Earth's atmosphere

I like airlines that have a lot of extra leg room

that have excellent service
that have good food
like pasta, beef, burritos, and sandwiches
I like plane rides that are five hours or less

I like getting mail from the airlines
I am a member of:
American's AAdvantage,
Delta's Frequent Flyer,
Northwest's World Perks,
TWA's Frequent Flight Bonus Program,
and Gold Ambassador,
and United's Mileage Plus

I have taken nineteen different airlines
and one hundred and sixty five airplanes

The airlines I have been on are:
Air France, Alaska, All Nippon, Aloha, American,
Continental, Delta, Hawaiian,
JAL, JAS, Lufthansa, NFD, Northwest, Pan Am,
Southwest, Swissair, TWA, United, and USAir

The aircraft I've been on are: Fokker 100s,
Airbus A320s and A300s,
Boeing 727s, 737s, 747s, 757s, and 767s,
McDonnell Douglas DC-9, DC-10s, MD11s,
MD80s, and MD88s, Lockheed L1011s,
and propeller planes

The destinations I've been to are:
In the United States:
Los Angeles, Burbank, San Diego, San Luis Obispo,
Orange County/John Wayne, Phoenix/Fort Rye,
Albuquerque, Portland, Seattle, Katchikan, Sitka, Honolulu,

Hilo, Denver/Stapelton, Dallas/Fort Worth, Lambert/St. Louis,
Detroit/Metropolitan, Minneapolis/St. Paul,
Milwaukee/Miffen, Chicago/O'Hare, Louisville,
Washington/Dulles, Washington/National,
Baltimore/Washington, Pittsburgh, Newark, New York/Kennedy
and LaGuardia, Buffalo, and Boston/Logan

Out of the United States:
San Juan/Luis Munoz Marin, Charlotte-Amalie, Christiansted,
Base Terre, Fort de France, London/Heathrow, Zurich/Kotell,
Basle/EuroAirport, Geneva, Amsterdam/Schiphol,
Frankfurt/Rhein Main Flughafen, Berlin/Tegel Flughafen,
Templehof, Nuremburg, and Tokyo/Narita, Tokyo/Haneda, Nagoya,
and Shin-Chitose in Sapporo

The airlines I think that are excellent are:
TWA, Lufthansa, American, Delta, Continental, JAL,
JAS, All Nippon, Air France, NFD, Pan Am, and Alaska
The airlines I think that are poor are:
United, USAir, Swissair, Southwest, NFD,
Hawaiian and Aloha

I like A320s, A300s, B747s, B767s, L1011s, MDDC-9s,
MDDC-10s, MD11s, MD80s and MD88s because they are big
wide bodied planes which makes them comfortable
I don't like B727s, B737s, B757s, and F100s,
and propellers because they are small,
narrow bodied and bounce a lot in stormy weather

I refuse to go on
propeller driven aircraft
because I think they are dangerous
every year there are about twice
as many commuter plane crashes
as big airliner disasters

I like the foreign airlines more than
most U.S. airlines
I have been on because
most foreign airlines have a very good safety record
the stewardesses are friendly,
they make their planes comfortable
and they put you up in
first class even though you pay
an economy fare

I don't like taking the cheap airlines
because it usually means that their maintenance
is poor and that their service is poor too

I have flown every year of my life
and every plane ride is different

I get very excited before a trip
I have been on airplane rides from
20 minutes to 13 hours
from as small as an ATR-72
to as big as a 747-400
I have flown as close as San Luis Obispo
to as far as Tokyo

POEMS MAKE YOUR LIFE BETTER

Poems make your life better
because you can express
your life
and feelings
on paper

You feel better
about yourself

People will listen
to the poems
and realize
what's going on
in the world

My poems
have taken me travelling
to Portland, Oregon twice
New York City,
Seattle, Los Angeles, and overseas,
to Potsdam, Bonn and Berlin Germany, Den Haag
and Eindhoven Holland

Poems got me on television
and the radio
and into the card catalogues
of libraries
where I can look up
my book by calling
up my name

So I've had my fifteen minutes
of fame and fortune

and I still feel
there are more poems to go
into a fourth and fifth book
in the poem folder
of my brain

Poems made my life better
so express yourself!

ABOUT THE AUTHOR

Tennessee (a Cherokee word for "the bend in the river") was born on February 28, 1977 at Kaiser Hospital in Oakland, California. Since the publication of her two poetry books, *Circus in the Sky* (I. Reed Books, 1988) and *Electric Chocolate* (Raven's Bones Press, 1990), Tennessee Reed has startled the literary world with her gifts and range. Her work appeals to people of all ages and has encouraged children to read and write.

The poems in her first book of poetry were written between the ages of five and eleven (kindergarten through fifth grade). The poems in her second book of poetry, *Electric Chocolate,* were written between the ages of eleven and twelve (sixth and seventh grades), and this third book, *Airborne,* was written from ages thirteen through nineteen (from eighth through twelfth grades and during her first year of college).

Tennessee Reed first read her poetry at the University of California at Santa Cruz, the Volcano Arts Center in Volcano, Hawaii, and Alaska Public Radio. To celebrate the publication of her first collection of poetry, Tennessee read at Cafe Milano, Cody's Bookstore, and KPFA radio in Berkeley, at the Exploratorium's McBean Theater in San Francisco, and on Bay area cable television programs.

Her second book of poetry took her traveling to the Portland Lit Eruption in Portland, Oregon, Harvard High School, Los Angeles, Barnard College and Mosaic Bookstore in New York City, Bumbershoot Arts Festival in Seattle, Washington, the San Francisco Bay Area Book Festival, and the University of Potsdam, Germany.

In June, 1993, Tennessee traveled to The Netherlands to participate in the Crossing Border Festival, reading her poetry in The Hague and Eindhoven. In October, 1994, she became the youngest artist to be sponsored by the United States Information Agency's Arts America program, reading her poetry in Bonn and Berlin, Germany.

At Merkin Hall, December 4-5, 1993, composer/musician Meredith Monk and her ensemble performed the New York City premiere of "Three Heavens and Hells," a twenty minute a cappella work for four female voices with text by Tennessee Reed. Ms. Monk has performed the work throughout the United States and Europe, and recently recorded it. The work had its world premiere at the 1992 Bay Area Dance Series, as part of *Face the Music,* a live video work created and performed by The Children's Troupe of Roberts and Blank. Composer Carman Moore set another of her poems, "Old Parents Blues," to music for the same event.

Her work is available at all branches of the Oakland and Berkeley Public Libraries and on audio tape at the Bancroft Library, University of California, Berkeley. Her work has also been published in the *San Francisco Examiner, Quilt* magazine, the *California State Library Foundation Bulletin, Poetry USA #25 & 26, The Raven Chronicles,* and *Konch* magazine. An excerpt of "The W Poem," appears in a Holt, Rinehart and Winston Grade 7 textbook, *Elements of Literature.*

Tennessee has grown up in Oakland and is now nineteen years old. She is in her sophomore year at Laney College. Whether writing about growing up, her grandfather's death, or the human heart, Tennessee Reed is exciting and original.